SCALAWAG

The Press *in* Prison

A practical, abolitionist
guidebook from *Scalawag*

 **Haymarket**Books

Chicago, Illinois

The
Press
in
Prison
The
Press
in
Prison
The
Press
in
Prison
The
Press
in
Prison
The
Press
in
Prison
The
Press
in

SCALAWAG · PEN AMERICA

A <u>Scalawag Media</u> guidebook for journalists.

Illuminating the need for incarcerated voices in journalism, this guide is intended to increase newsroom competency and capacity to work with writers on the inside, integrating reporting from prison into regular reporting cycles.

Edited by:
Lovey Cooper, Emily Nonko, & Danielle Purifoy

Additional support:
Ko Bragg, Sarah Glen, & Alysia Harris

Layout and design:
Virginia Walcott

Illustrations by:
Sydney Joslin-Knapp, Jesse Kruze,* Moyo,* Carla Joan Simmons,* & Tomás*

Artwork created by incarcerated and formerly incarcerated artists working with the Justice Arts Coalition

Table of Contents

Contributors

Christopher Blackwell

Christopher Blackwell is a writer serving a 45-year prison sentence in Washington State. He co-founded Look 2 Justice, an organization that provides civic education to system-impacted communities and actively works to pass sentence and policy reform legislation. He is currently working towards publishing a book on solitary confinement. His writing has been published by *The Washington Post, The Boston Globe,* HuffPost, Insider, and many more outlets.

Lovey Cooper

Lovey Cooper is the Managing Editor of *Scalawag.* She is based in Durham, North Carolina.

Arthur Longworth

Arthur Longworth is a writer at Monroe Correctional Complex.
Arthur Longworth has won six National PEN Awards and is the author of two books: *Zek,* and *The Prison Diary of Arthur Longworth #299180.* He has written for the Marshall Project, VICE News, and *Yes! Magazine,* as well as a wide selection of literary journals. Arthur's work has been read on stage at events in New York City by celebrated literary figures, Francine Prose and Junot Diaz, and American hip-hop artist and poet, Talib Kweli. His writing has been adopted into the curriculum of courses at the University of Texas, Santa Clara University, and the University of Washington.

Lyle May

Lyle C. May is a prison journalist, abolitionist, Ohio university alum, and member of the Alpha Sigma Lambda honor society. As he pursues every legal avenue to overturn his wrongful conviction and death sentence, Lyle advocates for greater access to higher education in prison. His fight is that of millions, and while the opposition is strong, his desire for equal justice is stronger.

Emily Nonko

Emily Nonko is a social justice and solutions-oriented reporter based in Brooklyn, New York. She is an organizer with Empowerment Avenue, a program supporting incarcerated writers.

Prison Journalism Project

The Prison Journalism Project is a non-profit, non-partisan national organization that trains incarcerated writers to be journalists and publishes their work.

Danielle Purifoy

Danielle Purifoy is an assistant professor of Geography at The University of North Carolina at Chapel Hill. She is the former Race and Place editor of *Scalawag*.

Jessica Schulberg

Jessica Schulberg is a senior reporter covering politics and the criminal justice system for HuffPost. Her work has also appeared in *The New Republic* and *The Washington Post*. She holds a master's degree in international security from American University.

Akiba Solomon

Akiba Solomon is an NABJ-Award winning journalist from West Philadelphia and a senior editor at The Marshall Project. A graduate of Howard University, she has served as senior editorial director at Colorlines and has written about culture and the intersection between gender and race for *Dissent, Essence, Glamour,* and *POZ*.

Jessica Sylvia

Jessica Phoenix Sylvia is an incarcerated transgender writer, community rganizer, and revolutionary abolitionist. She is also a philosopher and advocate for investment in global human development.

Rahsaan Thomas

Rahsaan "New York" Thomas is the co-host and co-producer of the Pulitzer Prize-nominated and DuPont Award-winning podcast Ear Hustle, as well as a contributing writer for The Marshall Project, Current, and *San Quentin News*. Additionally, he's a member of the Society of Professional Journalists and the co-founder of Prisonrenaissance.org—all from prison.

Jeffrey Young

Jeffrey Young is a Boston-born Cape Verdean who moved to Minneapolis at age 10 and graduated from Grambling State University in 2001. He is currently an associate editor for *The Prison Mirror*, the oldest continuously published prison newspaper, based in Minnesota's Stillwater Correctional Facility. Since 2011, Young has been an opinion columnist for *The Minnesota Spokesman-Recorder*, Minnesota's longest continuously published African American led newspaper. He is also a participant in the Minnesota Prison Writing Workshop program and a co-editor for an upcoming anthology about experiences with class differences, to be published by leading independent press Coffee House Press. He's a two-time winner of the annual PEN America national Prison Writing Awards for memoir and fiction writing categories.

1A. Freedom *of the* press in prison

Desire
by Tomás

ABOUT THE ART: "It seemed that everyday the newspaper arrived with troubling headlines about a deeply personal issue, immigration. My father illegally entered this country with his family when he was quite young. These news stories somehow felt like a threat to me and my family. These feelings lead me to transfer the newspaper articles themselves to a canvas around an icon of a Hispanic woman. She represents resilience and draws a parallel between our country and its people." – *Tomás*

If "prison" were a city, it would be the fifth-largest in the country, three times that of our nation's capital.

In journalism's heyday, it would call for at least two major daily newspapers, competing local television stations, and a public radio headquarters.

By sheer numbers alone, there is an apparent need for more journalism by and for incarcerated people. The impact of this coverage gap goes further than numbers can show.

Freedom of the press is the hallmark of a democracy in which the powerful are held to account. As journalists, our work implies a certain set of shared values. Chief among those for journalists who call ourselves watchdogs is a guarantee to shed light on systemic injustices.

The stymied flow of information to and from prisons facilitates abuses of power and the degradation of the very values we share. Continuing to ignore, sequester, and silence victims of the country's largest violator of rights is antithetical to our duty as responsible custodians of democracy.

Much like journalism itself, this guidebook also presumes a set of shared ideals:

Pursuing more comprehensive reporting that accurately—and responsibly—represents the audiences we serve requires new modes of recruiting, editing, and thinking.

This guidebook assumes you are willing to invest in meaningfully creating space for voices outside the traditional paths to journalism.

Reporters on the inside are deeply impacted by the system they report on—a fact of the reality imposed when living at the whims of a system as all-encompassing as institutional incarceration.

This guidebook assumes an understanding of this as proof of the value of stories that outside journalists simply cannot tell.

Publishing writing from prison is antithetical to the goals of the system that keep people incarcerated.

This guidebook assumes that all journalism is in service of the people, over institutions.

The unacceptable erosion of press freedom and diversity taking place in the public today has always been part of the lived realities of people on the inside. The details shared in this collection are intended to walk journalists on the outside through the considerations necessary to begin the process of breaking down those barriers. This work takes a special kind of initiative to start.

There are limitations to the tools at our disposal in the ongoing project of equality, just as there are with challenging any state-sponsored power. For instance, you may notice that this collection of resources primarily features writing from men. That inequity is partially due to the lack of equitable writing resources and support allocated to women's prisons. Similar to the material challenges you'll read about the process itself, this imbalance of voices is one of many tough realities that should not simply be solved with more funding, policy shifts, or governmental programs.

Don't let those realities discourage you. Rather, let them speak as an argument that the very work of publishing incarcerated writers requires an abolitionist framework. Challenging this system inherently means rejecting it.

The freedom of the press—everywhere— is essential for the future of our industry, and our democracy.

The pandemic and anti-policing movements may have started to warm the public to the concept that the prison industrial complex is inherently unsustainable, but every current crisis—from wage inequality to climate change—has been exacerbated behind bars. This country's fifth-largest "city" is full of knowledgeable, responsible watchdogs with stories to share. Pass them the mic.

"If the first task of the press is simply to be aware of its task, prison journalists as a whole would seem to rate high.

Despite the fact that many of them must produce their publications under conditions unimaginable to any outside editor or reporter with a pastepot to call his own, they nevertheless turn out some of the most relevant and responsible journals to be found anywhere. And the best of them, conscious of the special role of the prison press, express only two main concerns—that despite the accessibility of most prison publications, few outsiders are even aware of the job they are doing; and that, when the prison journalist is finally released, he will stand on an almost nonexistent chance of being asked to put [to use] some of the ruggedest and most valuable on-the-job training available anywhere."

— James F. Fixx, "Journalists Behind Bars" in *The Saturday Review*. March 9, 1963

1B. Doing the *(internal)* work

BY DANIELLE PURIFOY

My African American Stuck Dream by Moyo

Whenever a thin envelope arrived from Raleigh's Central Prison, I knew something was up.

Lyle's envelopes were typically pulling at the seams, thick with handwritten pages of essays and intensely researched articles on subjects like North Carolina's Racial Justice Act[1] or the state's parole laws.[2]

A one-page letter from Lyle typically meant bad news. Sometimes it meant that he had spent some part of the previous month in solitary confinement, or that his cell had been turned upside down by the guards. Worse, sometimes it meant that certain "privileges," like his education, had been stripped away indefinitely. There were times when this news would not arrive to me in the mail at all, but through an email from one of his friends or his academic adviser at a university several states away—someone who mostly knew him by phone, but who took care to send him reading materials by mail and instructions for proctored exams. Other times he'd give me a prepaid call: After I pressed "5" and the digital lady's voice said, "Thank you for using Global Tel Link," his first words might be, "Guess what happened?"

"They're just mad," I would say, apologizing. An incarcerated person who reads and writes is a threat to the prison industry as soon as they become uniquely able to disrupt its carefully crafted narratives about itself. As a legible, multidimensional person on the "outside," they suddenly undermine the prison system's premise that people can be disposable. Among the many things that solitary confinement is—including torture—it is a refusal to reconsider the social order that pays literal (and moral) salaries.

The prison officials' timing always made their retaliation clear. Lyle would write an article critiquing a law or a case, or a prison policy the newspapers never investigated or questioned, and a few weeks later I'd get a call, an email, or a thin envelope. He knew the price, and he wrote anyway.

My job as his editor was to make sure we at Scalawag publicly supported him[3] and his work, and to trust him to write the stories he thought were important—even if, as was often the case, no other outlets were covering them outside of prison.

If ever there was evidence that media objectivity does not exist, consider coverage of the prison system and those imprisoned within it.[4] Far more than mainstream coverage of civilian life on the "outside," which mistakes objectivity for viewpoints[5] that silence marginalized voices, prison journalism is often actively hostile to incarcerated people. Even in organizations with missions to "uplift" voices of incarcerated people, their practices often bely their stated intentions. Incarcerated people are most often presented to the world by the media as objects upon which to project public outrage and fear, even when they are published in their own voices. Think about it: Why would you publish an incarcerated writer's conviction/sentence in a piece about something unrelated to their charges? One way to make bad journalism is to build in narratives that deflect the reader away from the central subject of the writing. And yet, media outlets routinely require incarcerated writers to redirect public attention away from what they write about, and toward a value judgment of who they are and whether they can be trusted, because of some harm they allegedly caused.

Additionally, incarcerated writers are often pigeonholed into writing personal essays and opinion pieces rather than given the space for the fact-finding, investigative work required by journalism. While personal storytelling can be compelling, this practice frequently appeals to public voyeurism of "crime," and reinforces a presumption that incarcerated people cannot be trusted with holding accountable systems of power. These refusals result in media organizations uncritically accepting official statements and stories offered by prison officials and elected officers about everything from prison conditions to laws that impact incarcerated people.

If media organizations take seriously the mission to make even the most powerful institutions more transparent and accountable to the public, then building the press in prisons is a worthy practice. In four years of working with Lyle at Scalawag, I learned three major lessons about the unique and critical work of incarcerated journalists.

1. Build a relationship, not a sponsorship

It's all about building trust. Incarcerated people are under constant state surveillance and subject to arbitrary punishment. Making the decision to hold accountable an institution that has nearly total control over your life is both a personal feat and a tremendous public service. The prison industrial complex has a major influence on our society's cultural, economic, and political norms, values, and practices—with consequences that extend far beyond incarcerated people. All of our freedoms rely on how much power is wielded by this system. The best way to support this work is to support the person you're trusting to disrupt that flow, an act of solidarity that requires support far beyond mere "sponsorship." If a writer is going to take such large risks, editors and journalists on the outside must practice care, compassion, and reliability in the working relationship. Allocating additional resources to their projects and making time for phone calls and in person visits to build greater connections and community are benefits, not liabilities. I cannot say enough about how important it was to visit Lyle in person. Those visits transformed the nature of our work together. We could spend 2.5 hours talking about whatever was on our minds instead of 15 minutes rushing through a draft over the phone. We built trust and compassion for each other. We send each other holiday cards. Even though I'm not his editor anymore, I still go visit him now just to talk shit and see how he's doing.

2. Build a tailored ecosystem of support

The amount of labor required to drive an investigation inside of a prison cannot be underestimated. Prisons are designed to restrict the flow of information, to limit knowledge production. Incarcerated journalists often do not have access to the internet, have limited media and book access, and work in libraries that are notoriously lacking in resources. They often work by pen and paper and/or typewriter. Sustaining the work without undue hardship requires devoting time, resources, and people to back up the work. Make sure to make room in your organization's workflow for typing handwritten drafts, for sending and receiving feedback through mail, for lost or confiscated materials, for delays and public responses to retaliation, for phone calls you can't return, for conversations that need to be held in person rather than by phone, for setting up alternative systems of payment, for correspondence with sponsors and other supporters, and for backlash. These efforts are worth your organization's resources and time because they produce rooted and original journalism, because they can shift power within prisons, and because they can shape future narratives of the prison system outside of the system's control.

3. Build collaborations

Building relationships and ecosystems to support journalists in prisons might seem like a reason to keep the publications exclusive. Resist that urge. Build collaborations to share publications as widely as possible. You will reach greater audiences, and grow potential for greater impact, both in terms of public narratives about the prison industry and for much needed interventions. The journalists will likely enjoy more opportunities to write, and your organization will grow a reputation (and hopefully more resources) for continuing this important work.

2A. **Exploring the existing models:** *Ways to start working with incarcerated writers*

BY RAHSAAN "NEW YORK" THOMAS

Several times a week, I stand on a white-plastic bucket turned upside down and placed at the end of the top bunk.

Pressing my "flabs" (pot belly) against the edge of the bed, I flip the mattress in half, exposing the metal cookie sheet underneath. Then a typewriter gets placed there, and I start writing for various editors in the dim light of a prison cell. My completed stories get snail mailed to various publications. I am a contributing writer for Current, The Marshall Project, and San Quentin News, with numerous freelance credentials earned since June of 2020 at nearly two dozen other outlets. I became a frequently-published writer from prison because volunteers, organizations, and editors realized it's worth the extra effort to free the voices of incarcerated people.

Editors get several benefits from this work, too. Notably, they gain access to inside perspectives that have won awards. San Quentin News, UnCuffed, and the Ear Hustle podcast, all launched from San Quentin State Prison, are proof of our talents and the public's hunger to hear our voices. Working with journalists behind bars gives editors an avenue to give a voice to the voiceless. Incarcerated people have great insight and ideas into social justice issues that could better our society. And, it's the right thing to do if you want to live in a world without mass incarceration and violence.

For editors who want to make this investment, you're probably looking for a way to start. Here are some of the existing models that have worked for me.

Organizations focused on prison writing

The organizers of the Prison Journalism Project started out as volunteer instructors for the San Quentin Journalism Guild. I've had the pleasure of learning longform journalism from both Kate McQueen and Yukari Kane. Shaheen Pasha has also visited the newsroom and has taught journalism classes in Massachusetts prisons. Now PJP is out to spread the gospel of journalism to other prisons through the mail.

Additionally, Caits Meissner from Prison and Justice Writing at PEN America visited my creative writing class at San Quentin taught by writer Zoe Mullery. The proximity with incarcerated people gave PEN and PJP the inspiration to figure out how to mine the ink from our pens.

Exploring the existing models: *Ways to start working with incarcerated writers*

Empowerment Avenue

Without outside help to overcome a lack of email, Google, and connections to publishers, our voices remain stifled. Between 2013 and 2019, I managed to get published about eight times. Since the launch of Empowerment Avenue, a program I co-created with Brooklyn-based freelance writer Emily Nonko that pairs writers on the inside with accomplished writers in society, the gap has been closed between editors and cell blocks. Through Empowerment Avenue, I have been published 22 times since June of 2020.

The volunteers get us over the hump by transcribing our pieces into emailable documents that get sent out to editors. I work with Adrienne Gaffney, a free-lance editor for Elle Magazine. She facilitates conversations between me and editors who don't normally have access to incarcerated people or understand how to communicate with us. Through Adrienne, I am able to find out about writing opportunities, write for outside publications, and meet deadlines.

I envision Empowerment Avenue as a conduit for incarcerated people across the nation who write on a journalistic or advanced level to have their voices amplified in mainstream outlets. As the program grows, we hope to increase from 30 writers across the nation to hundreds and hit nearly every publication in America. (Email: empowermentave@gmail.com to get involved.)

Co-reporting

There are some stories I have been unable to write because I lack the ability to do research and conduct a full investigation. However, I do have something most publisher's don't—access to the people whose lives are impacted and mass incarceration and social injustice. To overcome those obstacles, I would love to co-report with journalists and editors.

Type Investigations, a nonprofit, has offered their help in conducting research on issues threatening the lives of incarcerated people. Many other organizations and editors decide to work with people in prison to expose and improve the system.

BY RAHSAAN "NEW YORK" THOMAS

Fellowship opportunities

Editors should offer people in prison writing fellowships to support and reward our work. My experience with the Marvel Cooke Fellowship, offered through the publication Shadowproof, is instructive. I received a JPAY letter from Empowerment Avenue telling me about the fellowship and applied. Thereafter, I connected directly with Brian Nam-Sonestein, the editor, and worked with him on a draft and the edits. The fellowship produced amazing results; I completed a piece for Shadowproof called "At San Quentin, Incarcerated People Organize for Safety as Transfers Spread COVID-19."[6]

Incarcerated journalist Juan Haines completed a similar fellowship with PEN on COVID-19, resulting in an op-ed published with the San Francisco Chronicle. A few days later, a judge tentatively ruled that prison officials acted with deliberate indifference in transferring men with COVID-19 to San Quentin State Prison.

Remember that incarcerated writers can only call you back at certain times, as phone access is limited.

The two major prison phone companies are GTL[7] and Securus.[8] Empowerment Avenue's guide for editors[9] outlines how to set up these profiles, deposit funds and add the facility and writer to your account:

- In all communication, a person's prison identification number is crucial. You will need this number to set up a phone account, send them a letter via snail mail, or write them a digital message through JPAY.
- You cannot call incarcerated people, and when they call you, phone numbers may come from an area code that does not align with the prison's location.

Stories from prison have to be somewhat localized, but they can also be regional with resources.

Rather than seeking a national story, try to plan around how to adapt localized reporting and storytelling that is connected to larger issues, with the help of editors who can do internet research.

When men in a Pasquotank prison submitted a letter about the deplorable conditions they were facing in North Carolina prisons in 2021, Scalawag editors saw throughlines between a letter published by women in a Raleigh facility in 1975.[11] With an editor's note, we drew connections from the current happenings in the county made famous when Andrew Brown was shot and killed by police to systemic state-level issues going back over 45 years.

Direct relationships

The volunteers and staff I've worked with for Empowerment Avenue, PJP, and PEN are awesome—however, it's also important for editors to work directly with incarcerated writers. Sometimes our volunteers, accomplished journalists in their own right, get overwhelmed by prolific writers. Editors dealing directly with incarcerated writers eliminates any potential hold up going through busy middle people, and offers the chance to establish relationships that can come in handy for future stories and employment references.

Currently, I'm working with Apogee Journal executive editor Alexandra Watson on an issue written entirely by incarcerated artists, and it's been a dream. She understands how to navigate the prison system including setting up video visits, sending JPay letters, and accepting prepaid calls. We've been able to work well together despite the challenges because she took the time to figure out the most important step toward our success—the various prison communication methods.

Working with incarcerated writers comes with obstacles, but knowing how to work around them makes it possible to reap rewards for both writers and publishers. Read a guide from Empowerment Avenue for more tips on working with incarcerated writers.[10]

2B. **The anatomy of a story:** *The interpersonal work of co-reporting*

BY CHRISTOPHER BLACKWELL & JESSICA SCHULBERG

Prisons Said It Was COVID Isolation. The Incarcerated Describe Torture.[12]

As the pandemic ravaged prisons and jails, officials opted to force people into inhumane solitary confinement. HuffPost spoke to some who described how they "nearly broke."

BY CHRISTOPHER BLACKWELL AND JESSICA SCHULBERG
PUBLISHED 10/13/2021

How we did it:

1. THE CONNECTION

Since working as an incarcerated journalist, I've been able to develop some very productive relationships with editors, including journalist Jessica Schulberg at the Huffington Post. At the beginning of the pandemic, she was looking for people in prison to help gather quotes for pieces she was writing. When we started working together, she was flexible and willing to explain her vision. Jessica understood my concerns on how my voice would be used, and made sure I was a part of the project—not just simply a subject within it. Her approach made it easy to build trust between the two of us.

When that story was done, she made an effort to remain in contact. We came to build a friendship. I was interested in writing about the harms caused in prison, and she realized that she had the ability to support me—lifting and allowing my voice to have the stage, as opposed to suppressing and gatekeeping. She connected me with other contacts of hers and we began to build a symbiotic relationship as colleagues in journalism. We had conversations around pieces we were thinking of writing and would bounce ideas off each other. If she needed support for a story, like being connected with other prisoners, I would help facilitate that, not just because I could, but because I trust her. Soon we decided to co-byline a piece.

Christopher

Jessica has always been willing to fight for my perspective, which is often silenced as an incarcerated individual. A topic we continuously talked about was the abuse of solitary confinement throughout the country as the pandemic ripped through prisons. We knew the harm being caused was damaging to the thousands forced to experience it in the name of protecting prisoners, and we wanted to do something about it. She pitched the story to her editor, emphasizing to her boss how important it was to have reporting from inside prisons. His support of our idea helped it become a reality. Whenever I published a strong solo piece, she'd take it to her boss and say, "This is the guy I've been telling you about," never missing an opportunity to promote the work I contributed to the field of journalism. Without her willingness to push for these opportunities, it's quite possible that our voices would have been left as nothing more than quotes accumulated by a free journalist.

Christopher

The advantages of working with Chris on a story like this are obvious: he has witnessed this problem unfold firsthand and can speak from experience to the lasting damage of solitary confinement. He is also an expert on the legislative efforts to reform solitary and the linguistic maneuvering corrections departments will use to tout supposed policy changes that don't make much of a difference on the ground. I'm grateful that my editor immediately got the value of partnering with Chris and allocated money from our freelance budget to compensate him fairly. [Editor note: Christopher was paid $1,100 for his work.]

Jessica

3. FIGURING OUT THE PROCESS

One of the biggest challenges we've had to work through is finding ways that we can reliably communicate. When we first started working together, I would often miss his calls and, of course, couldn't just call him back. When his unit was on quarantine or lockdown, he had very limited access to the phone, so if I missed his call, it could be a while until we could speak again. We dealt with this by having an agreement that I would stay glued to my phone Monday through Friday, from 9 a.m. to 6 p.m. If I know he is going to call on a certain day, I'll message him on JPay to let him know when I have meetings or calls scheduled so he can try to call outside those times.

Jessica

Because of the lack of technology and access to information in prisons, there were times we'd spend far more time working through our piece than one normally would. We laid the outline of our story out, going back and forth on JPay until we were both comfortable with the direction and message of the piece. Then we divided up the tasks in accordance to who had the ability to accomplish what.

Christopher

Thankfully, Chris has regular access to JPay, which has alleviated a lot of the communication challenges. JPay is also how we coordinate writing. Early in the process, we worked together over the phone to come up with a story outline, which I sent to him via JPay, with each of our names next to the sections we were taking the lead on writing. Then, he would send me his sections as he wrote them, and I would copy/paste it into a Google doc.

Jessica

BY CHRISTOPHER BLACKWELL & JESSICA SCHULBERG

4. COLLECTING AND SHARING RESEARCH

Once we had collected all the material we planned to work with, Jessica organized and printed everything out for me, and mailed it to the prison. We both read the material, highlighted the parts that we thought were impactful and shared those parts. We went back to our outline and decided if we needed to restructure anything.

Christopher

I find that Chris has so much expertise from his lived experience and advocacy work that he is able to write authoritatively on many topics, without relying as heavily on internet research as I would have to. And when he knows he wants to cite a fact that he can't recall from memory, he will tell me (or whatever editor is working with) how to search for it and where to add it to his copy.

Jessica

5. REPORTING IT OUT

I did interviews with prisoners who had been forced to suffer through horrible experiences with solitary, connected her with people I knew in other prisons, and offered resources like the intake handbooks that were handed out when prisoners entered solitary confinement under the claim of being placed in medical isolation. This showed how similarities between regular solitary confinement and the so-called medical isolation solitary were not all that different. This was a critical piece of evidence in proving our point that medical isolation was no different from regular solitary confinement, and honestly, these handbooks proved it to be worse. Jessica took on the task of doing interviews with experts on the outside, and the prisoners housed in prisons across the country.

Christopher

Whenever I started talking to another source about this story, they were always like, "Yes, yes, this is such a big problem, we're so glad you guys are covering it." I think the fact that I was working with Chris made sources—especially those in prison—have more confidence that the story would be told accurately and empathetically.

Jessica

6. WRITING THE PIECE

We each wrote our sections, and Jessica organized what we had written. I would send her my parts in pieces to be added to the overall piece. After it was written, we used JPay to go back and forth on minor edits. This allowed for her to teach me journalism techniques—like how to convey quotes in my own words, reminding me that I'm a professional writer and I shouldn't settle to use block quotes unless there's no way for me to word it better—and allowed me to educate her on areas in reporting on prisons, like the language we use to refer to people or things and why it's important to do so in that form.

Christopher

Once the draft was complete, I sent him a JPay message with the whole thing so he could read it over and flag any changes. JPay messages of that length take a long time to go through, so I try to also send a separate short message letting him know it's on the way. Because JPay messages are monitored, we only send things that we are OK with prison officials reading. That means not discussing names of sources via JPay unless they are comfortable being named in the story.

Jessica

When Jessica started fact-checking and reaching out for comment from places like the DOC, she made sure to run each part by me, allowing me to sign off before simply accepting a response. If pushback was needed, we crafted that message together. In the end, she was required to facilitate quite a few extra steps to keep me as an equal in the piece, but doing this allowed for us to grow and develop an amazing relationship as colleagues and the ability to learn from each side of the wall.

Christopher

BY CHRISTOPHER BLACKWELL & JESSICA SCHULBERG

7. THE IMPACT

There's a growing consensus that solitary confinement is bad and needs to be abolished or restricted. But what that translates to in policy and legislation is often pretty underwhelming. Some reform efforts only address "punitive" solitary confinement without touching other categories of isolation that are still punitive in effect. Others include explicit exceptions for medical isolation. Our goal was to show that locking people in a room for 23 hours a day—regardless of the intent— is solitary confinement and it is a torturous experience, no matter what you call it. We've been grateful to see anti-solitary organizers sharing the story and are hopeful that lawmakers and corrections officials are reading it as well.

Jessica

The hope is that our story will push individuals in society to see the harms being caused within prisons across the country. That even when it comes to incarcerated individuals receiving basic needs—medical treatment—in the thick of a global pandemic, we are instead abused and mistreated. The majority of the individuals behind these walls do not have a platform to voice the harms in which we are forced to suffer, but because of journalists like Jessica and her editor we were able to lift the voices of the voiceless.

Since our story was published I've received dozens of comments from my fellow prisoners thanking me for being willing to expose the harms we're forced to endure, and for risking myself in the process. I know I'm not alone in being willing to take a risk to change the destructive and extremely oppressive system over 2 million Americans call home. To bring real change, we need to lift the voices of the most impacted to have a seat at the head of the table. We do this by working together and offering opportunities to incarcerated journalists across the country the ability to speak about our environment.

Christopher

Where do you go to find incarcerated writers to work with? Think local.

Who in your community already works with incarcerated folks? Facebook and other support groups in your area can be a stepping stone to connect with loved ones on the outside to pass along information.

- Jessica got in contact with Christopher's wife after searching for people willing to speak about the difficulties of the pandemic as it progressed inside prisons. His wife provided her with his name and DOC number in order to connect over JPay. After messaging back and forth, the two eventually connected over the phone.
- To locate facilities near you, the website PrisonPath[13] offers a free search of prisons and jails at the state level, and the Federal Bureau of Prisons[14] has a tool for locating individuals within the system.
- To find a writer's prison ID, which you will need for all forms of communication, you can search their name through the state's Department of Corrections website.

Find incarcerated people who have already written about a certain issue you're interested in

Connected writers may have more contacts to point you toward.

- Check out PEN America's Prison Writing Award Winners Archive[15] to start.
- This year, The Society of Professional Journalists announced that they're partnering with the Prison Journalism Project to create a national, virtual chapter of incarcerated journalists serving time in correctional facilities across the country.

BY CHRISTOPHER BLACKWELL & JESSICA SCHULBERG

2C. **Nuts and bolts:**
*Best practices and
bad habits*

Human-centered language

The way language is used to describe the incarcerated is of great importance. As a society, we're finally starting to move into a direction where we are actively working to stop labeling individuals. Great efforts have been made to not label individuals by gender, race, and other relatable factors. The same respect should be given to the incarcerated. We're not offenders, inmates or convicts. We're human beings held in confinement—prisoners or incarcerated individuals/persons. If we plan to work as a society to not label those in our communities, we should do the same with those who remain confined in our prisons.
— *Christopher Blackwell*

During the editorial process, it's important to understand that many incarcerated people use neutral language and refuse to reproduce the language of the state. We don't refer to people as "inmates" or convicts," we call ourselves incarcerated people.
— *Rahsaan Thomas*

I sometimes feel offended at what I perceive to be outsider curiosity concerning the train wreck of being trans in prison. I do not need to hear how brave I am, and I do not want to be the object of pity. I appreciate respectful and humanizing interactions that involve dialogue. I feel best when publishing partners are willing to listen to what makes me feel supported. Let's remember to preserve people's dignity.
— *Jessica Sylvia*

The Marshall Project[16] *has developed a policy based on the logic of "people-first" language.*

"Originally developed by people with disabilities, people-first language avoids turning one aspect of a person's life into an all-encompassing label."

- Their policy is "designed to promote precision and accuracy and to convey the humanity of people who are routinely dehumanized by the media and society."

Communication

Editors need to go in understanding the rules of communication, which differs at different prisons. Some facilities allow tablets with email capabilities through the private service JPAY, while others can receive JPay letters within two business days, but can only respond through snail mail. Most prisons allow phone access, but you can't call the writer—we must call you, and you may need to set up a prepaid account with either Global Tel Link or Securus to accept the call. Understanding the rules of communication and planning ahead will give you the knowledge and tools to meet deadlines.

— *Rahsaan Thomas*

Provide multiple avenues for communication if possible, including email with the incarcerated person if that is an option, snail mail, and cellphone number of the editor for the incarcerated person to call during non-office hours, as that may be the only time available for a prisoner operating on the prison's schedule. If the incarcerated person is willing, it would be helpful if the editor had a phone number/email to a trusted loved one or friend of the incarcerated person to relay. Opportunities to check emails on prison tablet programs are sometimes limited, and opportunities to use the phone may be limited. An incarcerated person may have to choose who to communicate with in their short time out of the cell. Calling one's loved one/close friend who can also relay a message from an editor could be efficient and helpful at times.

— *Jeffrey Young*

Make sure you are checking out mail restriction policies. Depending on the state, there are limitations in the number of pages you can send, mail weight, ink color, type of paper and even whether you can send in double-sided pages. Most states prohibit stickers, which means you can't use return address labels and Post-its. Letterhead in color can also be a problem. If you violate any of the policy items, you risk the entire package getting sent back. In principle, PJP only sends letters and documents in black and white.

— *PJP editors*

If you're sending messages via the United States Postal Service, the website <u>IMailToPrisons</u>[17] offers a state-by-state breakdown of rules for sending certain kinds of mail.

From Empowerment Avenue's guide for editors:[18]
"Be sure you include their prison identification number in their mailing address. Be sure you include a good return address for them to write you back."

- As mail can be delayed by prison officials, dating letters will help an incarcerated person keep track of a letter's timing.
- If you plan to send source materials via snail mail, check with the writer first on any rules around mailing and receiving those items. Some facilities limit the amount of printed pages that can be sent or have restrictions on subject matter.

Timelines

When requesting work from an incarcerated writer, give as much lead time as possible. A writer in prison negotiates obstacles an editor or free-world writer likely can't fathom. I've had outgoing work confiscated for the following reasons: "Writing an article without Superintendent's permission," "Threat to orderly operation of the facility," and "Offender attempt profit from writing [sic]." Works in progress are sometimes destroyed or seized in cell searches. I often have to dictate drafts over the phone, or arrange for work to be smuggled out. An incarcerated writer is generally resourceful and determined; editors can rely on us. We simply face more obstacles than writers on the other side of the wall.

— *Arthur Longworth*

The Prison Journalism Project works with hundreds of writers across the country on stories that are published on our site, and we also help them pitch stories to outside publications where we see opportunities. One of the most important lessons we've learned along the way is that we have to factor in long lead times from the start of the project to completion. You have to overestimate shipping time, because prisons monitor incoming and outgoing mail. That process can take different lengths of time depending on the institution. When we send out mail, we usually factor in three to four weeks to get the first response. Even a JPay email could take 24 hours to reach. In Illinois, it could take three days before a prison greenlights an inbound electronic message.

— *PJP editors*

Communication monitoring

Even with the use of tablets, like all outgoing mail or electronic messages, our communication is highly censored, which can delay getting our pieces out in a timely manner. At times this will make deadlines almost impossible to meet.
— *Christopher Blackwell*

When you send mail, you have to be careful about how you word your correspondence. In some prisons, mentioning words like "warden" are automatically flagged for extra scrutiny. In others, sending in a W9 form could be problematic. Also make sure you are addressing the envelope correctly and written clearly. We have encountered prisons who send back mail if there is the slightest deviation from the way they ask mail to be addressed. Note too that the address for the prison and the address for "inmate mail" are often different. In Pennsylvania, for instance, mail is handled through a service in Florida.
— *PJP editors*

Nationally, more prison systems are increasing access to tablets, enabling more incarcerated people to respond quickly.

Empowerment Avenue's guide for editors[19] **outlines how to reach incarcerated people through electronic communications systems like JPAY.**

- Outlets should pay for the cost of a return "postage."
- Some prisons allow incarcerated people to respond via JPay, while others will have to respond via USPS or phone.
- If a writer can't respond to you via JPAY, be sure they have your address so they can respond via snail mail.
- Remember that communications are not private. Electronic messages and mailed letters may be read. Phone calls are recorded and monitored.

Bylines and convictions

Check with the incarcerated writer for what they would like their byline to look like. Some want their prisoner number or the prison they are in included, as it is a way for other editors/publishers to get in contact with them for more publication opportunities. Some are against any reference to them being incarcerated, so avoid adding "a prison writer/journalist" or "contributed by a prisoner" by default. Some may prefer the reference "incarcerated person" rather than prisoner. It is always a healthy choice to ask an individual how they would like to be referred to.

— *Jeffery Young*

We are more than the crimes that led us to prison. Using our crimes, victims, or their loved ones to entice readers is wrong. This has come up on more than one occasion with publishers, where I was pushed—even forced or threatened with losing the publication opportunity—to put why I was in prison or who I harmed to get here, regardless of the fact that none of the aforementioned had anything to do with the piece I was publishing.

—*Christopher Blackwell*

If your publication requires mentioning what crimes the person or author is in prison for, please discuss that up front. Things like language or crime may or may not be a deal breaker.

— *Rahsaan Thomas*

Reporting constraints

Each facility has unique restrictions that may seem random and arbitrary. Generally, higher security levels mean more restrictions. That means that greater accommodations may be needed for maximum security and segregated incarcerated writers. These writers may have difficulty even gaining access to pens, paper, and envelopes.

— *Jessica Sylvia*

Sudden lockdowns, transfers to another prison, or isolated quarantines can delay correspondence as well. This means that, for important stories, you should always have a contingency plan.

— *PJP editors*

Fact-checking and final reviews

When attempting to verify or fact-check an incarcerated writer's work, don't immediately defer to a state or prison official's denial or "alternative" version of an event. When I wrote that guards delivered mail for three days to a prisoner lying in a bunk deceased—tossing magazines, a TV Guide, and letters on the dead prisoner's chest—a prison spokesperson denied to VICE News that the event happened. The piece I wrote was stopped until, fortunately, I was able to provide the editor with a local newspaper article recounting the incident. Truth is often not aligned with what prison officials believe is their best interest. Be willing to dig a little to uncover the truth; don't be a sucker. And be fair to your incarcerated writer—share the prison's denial and/or statement with them.

— *Arthur Longworth*

The incarcerated should always have the ability to review and edit when appropriate final drafts and quotes. This ensures what's said isn't a misrepresentation of what they intended to write or say in an interview. One sentence can change our life drastically. Our safety and well-being should never come second in attracting readers. Stepping up to expose the inequalities of prisons and their administrations takes bravery. That should be respected, not overlooked.

— *Christopher Blackwell*

Reporting constraints cont.'d

We have limited ability to do research, and often have to rely on our support networks to obtain information to properly report and support our stories. We have very limited access to technology. Many of us do our reporting old school—paper and pen. Some prisoners have access to JPay, a service that allows prisoners to use small tablets to write and organize articles. These tablets are the equivalent of using your iPhone to write a piece with text-style typing. And often each state has different regulations and accessibility to the use of these devices, if they offer the use of them at all.

— *Christopher Blackwell*

2D. # How to pay incarcerated writers *for* their work

BY EMILY NONKO

Textile artwork above
by Sydney Joslin-Knapp
*Courtesy of Aimee Wissman**

Prisons intentionally make it hard for incarcerated people to earn money— sometimes through rules that prevent people from running businesses or carrying out a profession.

Writers earning an income is an active disruption to deeply entrenched structures that devalue incarcerated people's labor.

At the same time, it is important for editors to advocate for compensation with their editorial team and publication. Incarcerated writers should be paid comparable to any freelance writer doing similar work.

Even though prisons create challenges to fairly compensating incarcerated people, the work of writers is strongly protected by intellectual property law, which is protected by first amendment rights. Ultimately, the law is on the incarcerated writer's side—not the prison—when it comes to earning income off intellectual property.

Given these complexities, payment should be brought up early in the process in an open-ended manner. To avoid unnecessary risk or retaliation for the writer, you might want to position the conversation around pay as broadly and vaguely as possible. There are chances the writer will ask you to discuss the matter with an outside loved one who can accept money on their behalf.

Other writers might ask to be paid through transfer services like JPay or GTL; some writers have loved ones who hold outside bank accounts in their name. Payment will look different for everyone so it's important to get a sense of these unique considerations upfront.

BY EMILY NONKO

"I don't want to get into how we pay our writers beyond saying that I let them know that there is a 'small honorarium.' They often ask us to work with family members or other loved ones to secure the payment. Those discussions are vague since we know the communication is monitored. We're not doing anything wrong. We just don't want to draw unfair scrutiny at the facility level by talking at length about money." — *Akiba Solomon*

Bring payment into the conversation early

Given the variety of payment options, it's important to bring up payment, and how a writer can be paid, early in the process. You can position this in broad terms: "If we were to compensate you, how would you like that process to look?" and go from there. Be open to connecting with loved ones on the outside who might be able to talk more freely about compensation on behalf of the writer. If necessary, bring your accounts payable team into this discussion so you can be upfront and transparent about how your publication can, or cannot, meet requests.

"Compensate incarcerated writers fairly. That means no less compensation than you would proffer to an unincarcerated writer. This should be a matter of ethics for an editor, because an incarcerated writer may not know their worth. After all, it's easy not to know your worth when the people who run the institution inside which you're sequestered force you to work for nothing, or nearly nothing. And, contrary to whatever misconception is circulating out there about how everything in here is given to us, it isn't. Shit's expensive. I'm pretty sure I'm not the only incarcerated writer who has had to choose between buying needed hygiene items from the canteen or purchasing writing supplies and postage. I'm a writer because I chose the latter when I had to. Respect that." — *Arthur Longworth*

Outside bank accounts

Some writers have friends or family who hold outside bank accounts in their name. Other writers might be married and hold a joint bank account with their partner. In these cases, payment happens as it would with any writer—you send payment directly to their account, or send a check to the outside person connected to the account. You'll likely have to connect with that outside person to get the relevant information to make the payment.

More commonly, writers will have a friend or family member who is willing to accept payment on their behalf. In this case, you should check if your publication is willing to send the payment to that person, as opposed to the person who has written the story. If so, you can connect with that person directly to get information on how to send them a check or direct deposit.

Inside payment

For writers who do not have an outside account, or a person on the outside to accept money on their behalf, they can be paid directly— though it's likely you'll have to use a money transfer service, as opposed to sending a check directly. Money transfers happen through prison communication companies like JPay and Global Tel Link. Again, ask the writer what service their facility uses before trying to send payment.

Both JPay and Global Tel Link will require you, or someone on your accounts payable team, to set up an account before sending the money. These companies also will charge a fee for the money transfer. Sometimes these services will ask where you want the money directed. Be sure to direct the payment into the writer's commissary account, as opposed to restitution. When the money is dedicated to commissary, it means they'll have direct access to it.

BY EMILY NONKO

"It may not be an editor's responsibility to help writers file taxes, but it is a publication's responsibility to issue tax forms and any other necessary documentation in the course of doing business. This is an aspect of freelance work you might not consider when assigning stories, but it can cause headaches for any new writer. If you're paying more than $600 to a freelancer—regardless of if they're inside or outside—the IRS requires all businesses to issue a form 1099 for that payment. Your system might not know how to handle a sponsor versus a recipient, and neither may your writer. Be sure to bring this up at some point with your contributors." — *Lovey Cooper*

Circle back

Remember—an incarcerated writer does not have email to follow up on payment! It's important to stay in touch with your accounts payable team to make sure the payment went through successfully.

"When it comes to paying incarcerated writers, understand that the payment process looks different for us. It's important to get our payment information up front, especially since communication is so hampered. Also, know that we may require a degree of flexibility—many of us don't have bank accounts and may need a check mailed to our prison accounts or to a loved one." — *Rahsaan Thomas*

Our industry has a lot of work to do when it comes to pay transparency overall, but it's a particularly crucial topic when it comes to commissioning work from incarcerated writers.

Without the support of freelance networks that provide the opportunity for freelancers to "shop around," any writer without internet access relies on their editor to define fair compensation. Newsrooms should not only establish a policy around paying incarcerated writers, but one that is rooted in equity.

Scalawag's policy is to pay incarcerated contributors the same rate as any other writer. For an essay, that is a $600 flat fee. However, it's worth noting that many outlets have a policy to not offer pay for opinion pieces. Editors often mistakenly lump all writing from people in prison into this category by default in order to avoid some of the hurdles involved in payment.

Empowerment Avenue *writers shared a range of the rates they've been paid for essays, op-eds, and other first-person writing:*

- Solitary Watch's "Voices from Solitary" section: $25
- The Marshall Project & Life Inside: $50
- The Progressive: $100
- INTO Magazine: $150
- The Washington Post: $250
- The Boston Globe's "Ideas" section: $250
- THEM/Condé Nast: $300
- TruthOut: $350
- The New Republic: $400
- Business Insider: $500

BY EMILY NONKO

3A. On retaliation *against* incarcerated writers

BY LYLE MAY

As I opened that door I could feel the pieces of my shattered perception fall back into their respective place. I must remember that I am being punished, perpetually. Punished for riding in cars with boys, for being addicted to crack, for what Donnie did, for not really knowing Donnie, for what Donnie didn't even know he was capable of. For two decades there will be a punishment and if I, for even a moment forget, I will be reminded by the exploitation of my labor and talents, the confinement to closets and closet size spaces, and being made to piss with the rats. Shame is what they're after. It has sunk down into the very core of my being. It hangs in my clothes. It sleeps in my body. I am wholly defined by guilt and shame. The system pivots between being punitive and restorative and for the sake of rehabilitation inundates me with words like Character, Integrity, and Valor!,..... but never utters a thing about Dignity.

Scalawag published a piece I wrote, titled Prison officials cut off higher education for people on North Carolina's Death Row,[20] *in the Fall of 2019.*

The article shined a light of accountability on petty bureaucrats who decided to obstruct my access to privately-sponsored college correspondence courses. It was the kind of arbitrary, mean-spirited, and punitive decision that causes much of the dysfunction in North Carolina's prisons. An NCDPS official responded to the article on Scalawag's Facebook page, simply stating that my access to the correspondence courses had been restored. The internal response by prison administrators was not so polite.

A few days after the official responded publicly to Scalawag, an Internal Affairs (IA) Lieutenant and one of her staff locked me in a holding cell. Neither said a word and I was left to wonder if they were placing me under "investigation." Due process disciplinary rights suddenly become flexible or nonexistent when you are being investigated by IA, and many lose months in solitary confinement.

After an hour, the IA lieutenant and her staff left the unit without ever talking to me or the unit manager. I was released from the holding cell and told to return to my cell block. No one had answers for me, but when I saw my typically neat cell had been trashed—papers, books, clothes, and pictures littered the floor, sheets stripped from the bunk, chair turned over—I got the message: writing about prison officials has consequences.

In 1989, a federal appeals court[21] ruled that the First Amendment prohibits retaliation against prisoners for exercising free speech. In a later decision in which a man incarcerated in a Washington, D.C prison claimed a violation of his First Amendment rights, the U.S. Supreme Court[22] stated, "retaliation offends the Constitution because it threatens to inhibit exercise of the protected right." However, despite clear constitutional protections, covert retaliation still occurs because most prisoners lack the knowledge and resources to file a lawsuit. Some prison officials know this and use it to their advantage.

Prison accountability is what makes prison journalism critical to representing interests of the marginalized and oppressed, and why incarcerated writers put themselves at risk. The writing is less about individuals and more about examining policies and laws that fail to protect everyone in the system, with the goal of pursuing change. Prison officials often view this unwanted attention as a challenge to their control.

Retaliatory punishment is a common response to such challenges. Threats, harassment, revoked privileges, interference with the mail and access to the

Art on previous page: excerpt from *Shame* by Carla Joan Simmons

courts, destruction of property, hindered communication, solitary confinement, physical abuse, and transfer to more dangerous prisons in other states are just some of the retaliatory measures that have been taken against prisoners for exercising their right to free speech.

Incarcerated writers have to expect officials will ignore prohibitions against retaliation. The people who manage state penal systems are not held accountable often enough for anyone on the inside to believe the courts or public will assert any rights for the incarcerated. There are exceptions, like the <u>COVID-19 lawsuit filed in Wake County,</u>[23] North Carolina, or a <u>lawsuit to secure hepatitis C treatment</u>[24] for incarcerated people filed in one of the state's federal district courts in 2018.

Both lawsuits mandated access to adequate medical care in prison and requisite safety protocols because prison officials had refused to provide them. But these issues impacted prisoners as a class and were also tangible threats to public safety, which made them relatively easy wins for civil right groups filing class action lawsuits. Had these health issues just impacted people in prison, COVID-19 and hepatitis C would be running rampant in prisons. The problem with this standard of accountability is that one cannot accept help from the outside unless a civil rights group with their own interests is willing to take up the cause.

Otherwise North Carolina prisoners have to depend on an ineffective Grievance Remedy Procedure officials use to rubber stamp complaints, and on underfunded, understaffed Prisoner Legal Services that rarely pursue cases. As a result, the incarcerated suffer.

The risks associated with incarcerated reporting are worth taking because the public is ultimately responsible for what occurs within its prisons. Mainstream media narratives that regurgitate what state officials feed them cannot be allowed to dictate public perceptions of their incarcerated class. Editors stand as information gatekeepers who must be aware of their responsibility for fully informing the public, and the value of incarcerated writers in that process.

Media organizations protect and invest in the things they value. Any good editor will stand by their writers after a story has been published. Most editors, however, do not typically need to get involved with their writers' work when there is negative criticism. Most critics cannot punish writers with solitary confinement, billy clubs, degrading searches, destruction of their property, or longer prison terms through negative parole reviews because they exercised a right too many take for granted.

Standing by incarcerated writers does not have to mean an editor must file a lawsuit if public officials inhibit, retaliate against, or otherwise silence free expression. But some public officials are hardheaded and power hungry. "Please stop" will not be enough. The point is to call them out publicly every time, not just when it is convenient. Address them on social media, call them up directly, and write follow up articles that address the image they have of their position of authority. However it is done, a demonstration of support in the face of opposition can be enough. Support can take many forms, and it's a good feeling to know someone has your back, that you are not alone in the fight. Accountability is a community in action, serving the interests of its members, and providing strength in numbers. It's the only way to bring about lasting change.

> "When an incarcerated journalist exposes what's happening within the prison they're confined, they're taking a great risk. Rarely is the Department of Corrections (DOC) comfortable with having their dirty laundry aired out. DOC has spent decades controlling the narrative around what happens inside their prisons because of this, incarcerated journalists can face varying levels of retaliation. Some are small, while others can be devastating. I've personally had my incoming and outgoing mail delayed for weeks, and in rare cases thrown away. This made getting my voice out there extremely difficult and added high levels of pressure within personal relationships. Reporting from prison is equal to any journalist reporting from a hostel environment—reporting behind enemy lines."
>
> — *Christopher Blackwell*
>
> "If an advocate is pitching a piece on behalf of a person with lived experience, I specifically ask them about the person's physical/ administrative safety. I also explain how we fact check. I haven't had a problem with advocates enlisting people who don't want to be a part of the process."
>
> — *Akiba Solomon*

3B. Developing a career from prison:
It takes a team

BY LYLE MAY

Higher education gave me an edge when submitting my first article for publication to Scalawag.

Where someone less knowledgeable in essay writing might have struggled with structuring the argument, organizing information, and using sound logic, I found it normal. This gave me confidence. Drawing from lessons learned in writing and rhetoric, and from literary masters like George Orwell, I recognized my advantage. Accordingly, my first Scalawag article advocated for greater access to higher education in prison. Being a trained writer, however, is only part of the publication process.

Publishing while incarcerated is hard. Lack of access to computers or the internet or even a typewriter means handwriting (and carbon copying) submissions, then waiting on snail mail. Most publishers don't accept handwritten manuscripts, so you have to send out the work to be typed and mailed again. Research and revisions are similarly difficult. After putting forth so much effort, receiving a form letter rejection is discouraging.

My first rejection came with a note explaining how seldom the organization published, the many submissions by great writers that are turned down, and encouraged me to keep trying. No signature, feedback, or guidance. I was left to wonder if I had an awkward tone, the wrong politics, was the wrong topic or just bad writing. Maybe my lack of résumé and imprisonment were the only causes for rejection they needed.

Whatever the reason, rejection is part of the writing process. Stephen King impaled his many rejections on a nail in the attic where he wrote Carrie. Success in a writing career demands practice, determination, creativity, and resilience. Though the author gets the credit, publishing only happens with help from other people.

I knew early on that publishing a few essays about my experiences on death row and in prison would not be enough. I felt an overwhelming need to counter the one-sided sensationalism of mainstream journalism that typically excludes incarcerated voices and experiences. I wanted to challenge "official" reporting on North Carolina's penal dysfunction, which too often fails to hold state officials accountable.

"Career" had not made it into my lexicon when at a visit with Danielle, my first Scalawag editor, we discussed where I saw my writing going.

"I want to be the one you rely on for an insider's perspective," I told her. Most newspapers don't, or only describe us as a living extension of a crime. We have no representation in the media and I want to change that."

My familiarity with prison journalism came from Wilbert Rideau's and Kerry Myer's work on *The Angolite*, Erlonne Woods' and Nigel Poor's work with "Ear

Art on previous page: excerpt from *Shame* by Carla Joan Simmons

Hustle," and several independent writers whose work frequented PEN America collections and The Marshall Project. But the writing largely focused on infamous prisons, and lacked coverage of thousands of facilities throughout the U.S. labels like "inmate" and "offender" were attached to writers, their criminal conviction listed at the end of an essay like an asterisk.

It frustrated me to think there are journalists in every town of America, their names in print without a qualifier, but not in its prisons. In 2012, journalist Gary Fields[25] said, "Each prison is a fiefdom, and the warden is at the top of the feudal system." Fields covered criminal justice policy and practice for The Wall Street Journal and was explaining the difficulties of reporting on the inside from the outside. Several U.S. Supreme Court decisions over the last 40 years have restricted press access in prison, making it unlikely they can accurately cover what happens in a given facility or penal system. Without incarcerated writers and their first hand experience, reporting about the criminal legal system and mass incarceration carries the odor of propaganda. It takes editors willing to be inclusive, and not accept state officials' word as gospel or parrot state-reported statistics to award this fatal journalistic flaw.

There is no shortage of material to write about in prison because it is an authoritarian society sponsored by an apathetic democracy. It's more about choosing the most important and timely topics. Danielle made pitching topics easy by trusting my experience and judgment.

When it came to revisions she was not heavy-handed and explained why a paragraph needed to be moved or cut or restructured. Though I knew a lot about the politics of mass incarceration, policies of the criminal legal system, and life in prison, she reminded me that good journalism is story-driven. It was the kind of instruction I needed to become a better writer.

Citing sources of information is an ordinary part of any article, but fact-checking takes an added importance for prison journalists. It's good to be meticulously grounded in facts because an incarcerated writer's integrity will always be in question. Citing facts and their sources makes editorial support easier, and harder for prisons to assail or censor the writing. Challenging the penal narrative from the inside carries an inherent risk few other journalists in America experience, which is why strong editorial support is critical, far beyond the writing process.

In 2018 Scalawag published my article, "Measures Meant to Make North Carolina Prisons Safer do the Opposite."[26] After five guards were killed in 2017, prison officials "cracked down" on the incarcerated population. Draconian policies and vindictive officials cut much-needed rehabilitative programs, harassing an already frustrated group of people. From minimum custody facilities to death row, an increase in tension caused more assaults. These did not make the news. Instead, corrections officers were characterized as law en-

> "Being a freelance writer from prison has been life changing. For 19 years, my mother sent this grown man care packages and helped take care of my sons. Finally, I earn enough to take care of myself and help them out. Moreover, I feared coming home with gray hair and thousands in debt to court imposed restitution with absolutely nothing saved for retirement or coming from social security. The income from freelancing helps me prepare for success on parole and retirement. Best of all, I'm contributing to conversations around social justice in publications that reach beyond the choir."
>
> — *Rahsaan "New York" Thomas*

forcement heroes who did no wrong. Prisons were understaffed—not overcrowded. The responsibility for prison violence belonged to violent inmates, not a complete lack of incentives, antagonistic guards, or penal mismanagement. After publication of my article I received a not so subtle threat from unit management:

"You need to get your story straight. What you wrote is wrong. It wasn't in the news so it didn't happen like that. You think you have it hard? It can get a lot worse."

I told Danielle about the interaction and she was ready to provide whatever help she could. It reassured me to know the support went beyond an awareness of the risk from prison journalism. Scalawag has a genuine interest in representing marginalized people. Danielle's concern was not curiosity, charity, tokenism, or mutual benefit—she cared what happened to me as a human being, friend, and member of the Scalawag team.

What more can a writer ask for then to be represented and taken seriously by an editor? Professional treatment produces professional outcomes. The same cannot be said if the writer is treated as less than, a distraction, or someone whose ideas are good enough to misappropriate, but not receive credit.

A recent experience showed me the difference between the good editorial communication and support I receive from Scalawag, and the poor communication I received from a national newspaper. Some friends arranged a meeting with a journalist and two editors. I was asked to prepare several pitches in advance of the meeting, to be forwarded to the editors through the journalist. The phone meeting went well and the editors assigned

BY LYLE MAY

an article with a two week deadline for an initial draft. Within 10 days, I submitted a draft, followed by revisions three days later. That was it. I never heard back from the editors and they ignored emails from my friends. I had been dismissed with silence.

What happened to me is likely common, especially for incarcerated writers. It was infuriating and depressing, but not the end of the world. After all, rejection and opposition is the air we breathe in prison, and one develops a certain amount of resilience that cannot be overcome by a professional snub. Danielle commiserated with me even as she celebrated the potential of publishing with the newspaper. It's the kind of professional support and communication that has helped me flourish as a writer.

Stability enables innovation. The accessibility of Scalawag's online format made it easy to share my articles with criminal justice students. In 2018, I began speaking events with undergrad classes at UNC Chapel Hill, Ohio University, and the University of Minnesota at Minneapolis. Students were assigned some of my Scalawag articles, and over the course of two 15 minute phone calls, my voice amplified by a speaker in the classroom, I answered questions about capital punishment, executions, life imprisonment, higher education, penal reform, and criminal justice policies. By Spring 2021, with the aid of Zoom, I connected with a number of private high schools, church groups, podcasts, and over a dozen professors at eight different universities for a total of 50 speaking events. My writing for Scalawag and other publications became a platform from which I could teach the public about the myths and misperceptions surrounding crime and punishment.

It takes a special level of determination to keep learning and striving as a writer in prison. If success is defined as publication, this is unlikely without the help of friends or family at some point. Similarly, developing a successful writing career takes a special level of interest from editors who recognize and cultivate a writer's potential. All of it requires mutual respect and hard work. None of it happens without support on the outside. Writing in prison was never meant to be an isolated practice; it is a community-building event that takes a team.

3C. Editors' power *to level the* playing field

BY JESSICA SYLVIA

Untitled
by Jesse Kruze

Editors' Note

When we talk about prisons, we often center the men incarcerated in them. The lion's share of people incarcerated in the U.S. are held in men's prisons. And while women are being incarcerated at nearly double the rate of men, we almost never center their experiences. Jessica Sylvia reflects on this gap, and the ways we can better support people incarcerated in women's prisons. She wrote this essay from solitary confinement in Washington State, with limited access to pens and paper.

Female writers are greatly underrepresented in the writing program I am a part of, Empowerment Avenue.

When I see so many great stories written by men, it's no wonder I ask where the women are. We must work in order to create equal opportunities for women.

I am in a unique position as a transwoman forced to survive in a men's prison. I see how men are often the first to get access to the limited support offered inside carceral environments, and the resulting competition for resources. I am often left behind for support inside a male-dominated environment.

Support is even more lacking inside women's prisons than it is in men's facilities, despite the incarceration rate growing 700 percent in the last 40 years. Women's prisons tend to have lower visitation capacity and fewer opportunities for programming. Women in the system in general also tend to receive less individual support. Race, class, and gender impact most aspects of life, informing my analysis of how poor women of color are left behind.

Most women in our prisons are women of color who have experienced poverty. According to the ACLU,[27] nearly 60 percent of people in women's prison nationwide—and as many as 94 percent of some women's prison populations—have a history of physical or sexual abuse before being incarcerated. There are far too many women in prison for crimes directly related to abuse that they experienced. As a transwoman in a men's prison, I am 13 times more likely to experience sexual violence than average prisoners. Incarcerated women are survivors.

There has been much attention focused on how state sanctioned violence impacts men—and for good reason. Now, who is showing up for the women?

My hope is that my writing effectively illustrates the need to show up for women as I capture how generative and powerful sustained efforts can be. Awareness and visibility can lead us to build relationships that produce the type of solidarity needed to deliver justice to incarcerated female writers.

I cannot speak for all women, but I can voice the ways that editors I've worked with could better show up for me and other women:

Editors' power *to level the* **playing field**

Considerations

1. Before selecting a writer for a story, be sure to consider offering the opportunity to a woman.

2. Be intentional to include women of color, trans, and gender-non-conforming people. Historically, those identities have been marginalized or erased under the umbrella of "women."

3. Be nuanced enough to publish a variety of stories with a woman's perspective and voice.

4. Plan for news cycles: Plan to run women's stories in the coming year and make opportunities known well in advance, making accommodations for "prison time" because it takes longer to get things done in prison. We create more opportunities by not missing the moment.

5. Explore how gender-based violence and the carceral state play a role in harming and imprisoning women. Publish stories that help women while not exploiting their trauma for entertainment.

6. Pay women equally. Toni Morrison once said, "I'm head of household too." Women are not only paying for their needs, many are trying to support children, fund visits, and save for release.

Communication

1. Make time and space for communication to happen. Ask women what they need and how they feel about the process.

2. Have the awareness and sensitivity to recognize when a particular story may feel voyeuristic, invasive, or exploitative. Get expressed consent and avoid coercion. As a transwoman I sometimes feel violated when my trauma appears to serve as entertainment for readers while providing no support or justice for me in the end.

3. Remember to accept feedback and learn with women as you teach. Unique perspectives may surprise you by offering unique brilliance.

BY JESSICA SYLVIA

> In the interest of equity, some additional work may be necessary to help women catch up to male counterparts. Show women you believe in them by supporting and empowering them as they work to build skills and believe in themselves. If a woman lacks capacity to meet your needs and expectations, work with her to form a plan to get her on a pathway to success. A no today can be a future yes if we make intentional investments.

Continue to evaluate processes and relationships. Work to fearlessly confront failures while building on success.

Remember that this work is about much more than stories. We are working to support and empower women as we amplify their voices in the present with a vision of a more just future where women write themselves into history, making their work available to the next generation of women.

Writing from prison is hard. It's even harder for women, but editors have power to help level the field.

More than 70 percent of women who are incarcerated have been subject to sexual and/or domestic violence. A first step toward equity is to begin building relationships with organizations that work with survivors support incarcerated and formerly incarcerated women, as well as queer and gender nonconforming writers and artists.

- Black & Pink[28] and Exchange for Change[29] are a few of the organizations that work specifically with women who write behind bars.
- Research the work of organizations like API Chaya,[30] California Coalition for Women Prisoners,[31] Collective Justice,[32] Mothers on the Inside,[33] and Women on the Rise[34] to learn more about the compounding realities of gender-based violence and incarceration. Consider publishing a Q&A or profile on similar organizations.

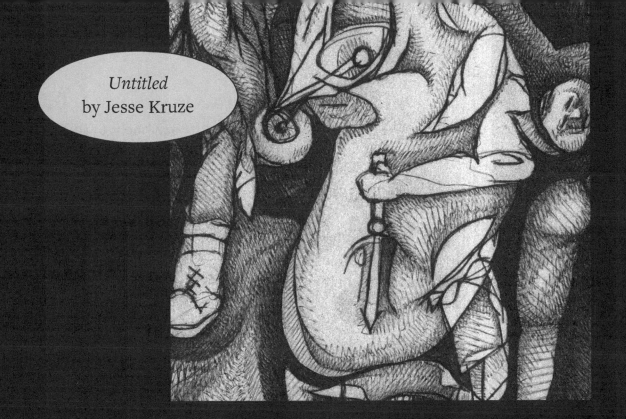

Untitled
by Jesse Kruze

4. Sustaining the work long term: *More resources and next steps*

The creativity, flexibility, and persistence needed to do this work was on display as we designed this guide.

The process of creating it was also a lesson in the political and logistical challenges we outlined. Jessica Sylvia's essay was written from solitary confinement, without access to her JPay tablet and limited access to pens and paper. She sent her draft handwritten through snail mail, which we transcribed to create a digital copy to share among this guidebook's editors before going over edits through a series of phone calls—calls that we were unable to pre-schedule. Rahsaan Thomas sent his edits through JPay, through messages that the administration at San Quentin simply prints and delivers by hand. In a phone call, he told us he never received the last draft we sent, so we went over the final details by phone after paying to send it again. Rights to reproduce the illustrations in this guide were procured largely through second-party liaisons, using four different methods of contact. In October, North Carolina's prisons started outsourcing their mail system to a private company called Text Behind, based in Maryland.[35] This meant that sending typed edits to Lyle May took several more days than it would have under the previous local system.

As editors, while we tried to make our coverage comprehensive, we must still acknowledge that this collection of pieces is missing a diversity of voices and perspectives from people currently reporting from prisons. We wanted to include the voices of incarcerated reporters at The Angolite, a prison newspaper with an incredible history, but the writers at Angola Prison do not have access to JPay. We sent a snail mail letter to the newsroom but did not hear back. It's likely the letter never made it to the newsroom in the first place.

Our main task with crafting this guidebook was to demonstrate the worth and value of working with incarcerated writers. Without their contributions, the public will continue to miss the ways that all of us—the media included—are complicit in upholding the prison-industrial complex. We know that we don't have all the answers, but we encourage you to join us as we sometimes run, sometimes stumble toward a more just world.

With this guide, we set out to help break what can be a daunting task down into consumable considerations. We believe that our work serves as a step in the right direction toward making working with incarcerated writers a regular part of your news cycle, too. To that end, here are some easy steps you can take today:

Start by getting your mailing address into prisons.

List off information about your publication, what kinds of stories you're looking for, and how to contact you. The Journal of Prisoners on Prisons[36] offers a solid sample submission guide to build to your publication's specifics. Put an editor in charge of reading and responding to those pitches.

Here are a few existing publications distributed in and from prisons to start with:

- Prison Legal News[37]
- San Quentin News[38]
- News and Letters Committees[39]
- The Inside Books Project Resource Guide for Inmates and the Families of Prisoners[40]
- Prisoner Express[41]
- Political Prisoner News[42] via the Freedom Archives
- Black And Pink's Penpals & Newsletter[43]
- Solitary Watch's Print Edition[44]
- The Abolitionist – A Publication of Critical Resistance[45]
- Justice Denied – The Magazine For The Wrongly Convicted[46]
- The American Dissident[47]

1.

Dive into your own content.

Get an intimate understanding about how some of the reporting your newsroom produces may be harmful to people impacted by the criminal-legal system: Who are your sources? How are you fact-checking cops and carceral officials? Are you still using the word inmate? An evaluation of your existing content can help give you a sense of how all of your stories—not just those you produce with incarcerated writers—can be aligned towards justice and equity. For a thorough report on carceral harms exacerbated by biased reporting, review the Texas Center for Equity and Justice's *The Real 'Bond Pandemic': Misinformation, False Narratives, and Bias in the Media.*[48]

2.

Volunteer your time.

Are you a freelancer? Volunteer your time with organizations that work with incarcerated writers and artists. Help <u>Prisoner Express</u>[49] type up and transfer over content that's sent in by hand. Join a writing mentorship or pen pal program with <u>Pen City Writers</u>.[50] Sign up to be an outside volunteer with <u>Empowerment Avenue</u>.[51] <u>Justice Arts Coalition</u>[52] needs volunteers willing to work with incarcerated artists as well.

3.

Set up your infrastructure.

Take an afternoon to create a JPay and Corrlinks account, either individually or for your newsroom. Making these profiles preemptively will be one less hurdle you have to overcome after you begin working with writers. By having multiple members on your team with access to multiple platforms, instead of relying on only one system, it will be easier to work with writers who may only have access to one or the other.

4.

Nurture existent careers in journalism.

While sourcing new writers requires a deeper investment, there are incarcerated writers who are already knowledgeable veterans of the process and are looking to work with more outlets. Support their careers by reaching out to offer them bylines in your publication. Make a commitment to contact two established writers whose articles piqued your interest, either via snail mail or through your newly-formed JPay account.

5.

Set up a budget meeting with your Managing Editor or Editor in Chief.

A small newsroom might set a goal of publishing four or five stories a year by incarcerated writers. If you are a larger newsroom, consider what it might look like to start working towards a goal of one story a month. Build a budget that pays incarcerated writers according to your current pay rates for freelance reporters. From there, you can build in additional funds for editorial time, resources, and support.

6.

Partner up.

Is there an organization that you often partner with or republish stores from? Talk to them about partnering for a series of stories over the next six months or year. Agree to co-publish stories by incarcerated writers coming out of both of your newsrooms to amplify the content's reach—and share editorial responsibilities. An arrangement like this can increase accountability and capacity to continue sustaining this work.

Don't underestimate the value of this effort. Institutions won't get us free, but collective action will.

Start small and stay consistent.

Thank you for your time. Feel free to reach out with any questions: editors@scalawagmag.org

Links

1 https://scalawagmagazine.org/2020/10/nc-rja-death-row-racism/

2 https://scalawagmagazine.org/2018/12/life-without-parole-is-silent-execution/

3 https://scalawagmagazine.org/2019/10/prison-education/

4 https://scalawagmagazine.org/2020/06/journalistic-freedom-on-death-row/

5 https://press.uchicago.edu/ucp/books/book/chicago/V/bo29172094.html

6 https://shadowproof.com/2021/09/29/at-san-quentin-incarcerated-people-organize-for-safety-as-prison-transfers-spread-covid-19/

7 https://web.connectnetwork.com/

8 https://securustech.net/

9 https://docs.google.com/document/d/1E_umpvWZZWJTpRSgwpw6bTlgN0RNljlm7rClY9X9Zoo/edit

10 https://docs.google.com/document/d/1E_umpvWZZWJTpRSgwpw6bTlgN0RNljlm7rClY9X9Zoo/edit

11 https://scalawagmagazine.org/2021/06/from-the-inside-letters/

12 https://www.huffpost.com/entry/medical-isolation-solitary-confinement-prisons-jails-pandemic_n_615f2f01e4b02bd79fbca775

13 https://prisonpath.com/

14 https://www.bop.gov/

15 https://pen.org/prison-writing-award-winners-archive/

16 https://www.themarshallproject.org/2021/04/12/what-words-we-use-and-avoid-when-covering-people-and-incarceration

17 https://www.imailtoprison.com/U-S-State-Prisons-Information_c153.htm

18 https://docs.google.com/document/d/1E_umpvWZZWJTpRSgwpw6bTlgN0RNljlm7rClY9X9Zoo/edit

19 https://docs.google.com/document/d/1E_umpvWZZWJTpRSgwpw6bTlgN0RNljlm7rClY9X9Zoo/edit

20 https://scalawagmagazine.org/2019/10/prison-education/

21 https://casetext.com/case/thomas-v-evans-3#p1242

22 https://supreme.justia.com/cases/federal/us/523/574/

23 https://law.justia.com/cases/federal/district-courts/north-carolina/ncmdce/1:2018cv01034/80757/140/

24 https://www.acluofnorthcarolina.org/sites/default/files/field_documents/buffkinvhookscomplaintfiled.pdf

25 https://www.quill.spjnetwork.org/2012/08/07/foi-toolbox-31

26 https://scalawagmagazine.org/2018/10/death-row-therapy/

27 https://www.aclu.org/other/prison-rape-elimination-act-2003-prea?redirect=prisoners-rights-womens-rights/prison-rape-elimination-act-2003-prea

28 https://www.blackandpink.org/

29 https://www.exchange-for-change.org/

30 https://www.apichaya.org/

31 https://womenprisoners.org/

32 https://www.collectivejusticenw.org/

33 https://www.facebook.com/Mothers-On-the-Inside-100334141816310/

34 https://www.womenontherisega.org/

35 https://www.ncdps.gov/our-organization/adult-correction/prisons/offender-mail

36 http://www.jpp.org/documents/forms/Submission_Guidelines.pdf

37 https://www.prisonlegalnews.org/advertise-with-us/

38 https://sanquentinnews.com/

39 https://newsandletters.org/

40 https://insidebooksproject.org/resource-guide

41 https://prisonerexpress.org/

42 http://freedomarchives.org/mailman/listinfo/ppnews_freedomarchives.org

43 https://www.blackandpink.org/penpal-newsletter/

44 https://solitarywatch.org/print-edition/

45 https://abolitionistpaper.wordpress.com/

46 http://justicedenied.org/index.htm

47 http://www.theamericandissident.org/

48 https://www.texascje.org/system/files/publications/2021-10/real-bond-pandemic-report-texas-center-justice-and-equity.pdf?eType=EmailBlastContent&eId=dc30630a-c515-4411-8580-7b040b513c1f

49 https://prisonerexpress.org/volunteer/

50 https://liberalarts.utexas.edu/english/programs-and-projects/pen-city-writers.php

51 https://www.prisonrenaissance.org/empowerment-avenue-writers-cohort

52 https://thejusticeartscoalition.org/

ISBN 978-1-64259-894-0

51500

9 781642 598940